The
Derbyshire
Heritage
Series

John Merrill's - "My Derbyshire" Historical Series.

Churches of Derbyshire

by
John J. Anderson

ISBN 0 946404 30 5

2000

The Derbyshire Heritage Series

Walk & Write Ltd.,
Unit 1, Molyneux Business Park,
Whitworth Road, Darley Dale,
Matlock, Derbyshire.
England.
DE4 2HJ

Walk & Write Ltd.,
Unit 1,
Molyneux Business Park,
Whitworth Road, Darley Dale,
Matlock, Derbyshire
DE4 2HJ
Tel/Fax 01629 - 735911

First Published - 1984
Reprinted - February 2000

ISBN 0 946404 30 5

British Library Cataloguing-in-Publication Data. A catalogue record of this book is available from the British Library.

Typeset and designed in Garamond - bold, italic, and plain 10pt. 12pt, 14pt and 18pt. by John N. Merrill.

Cover design © Walk & Write Ltd 2000.

ACKNOWLEDGEMENTS

Acknowledgements are due to the incumbents, vergers and churchwardens who have helped. To the staff of the Derby Local Studies Library and the Derbyshire Local Studies Depatment for unfailing courtesy and assistance and not least, to my wife whose patience and endurance has been a constant source of encouragement.

Much information has been gleaned from these suggestions for further reading.

Bygone Derbyshire	Edited, Andrews
Dictionary of National Biography	Editors, Stevens & Lee, Williams & Nichols
Derbyshire Collection 4686	Derby Local Studies Library
Derbyshire Records (Hunter)	Derby Local Studies Library
Derbyshire Archeological Review (Vol. XXI)	Edited, Jewitt
History and Antiquities of the parish church of St. Mathews, Morley	Rev. Samuel Fox
History of Derbyshire	Lysons (Derby Local Studies Library)
History of Leicestershire Vol. 3 part 2	Nichols
History of Derbyshire	Editors, Catherine Glover & Philip Riden
History of Colwick Abbey	Mary Teresa Fortescue
History of Derbyshire	William Wooley
History Gazetteer and Directory of the County of Derby Vol. 1 part 1 Vol. 2 part 2	Stephen Glover
Illustrated Glossary of Architecture	John Harris and Jill Lever
Notes on the Churches of Derbyshire	J. C. Cox
Notts. and Derbyshire Notes and Queries (Vol. 3)	Edited, Peter Briscoe
Old Halls, Manors and Families	Edited, J. T.
Parish Churches	J. C. Cox and C. B. Ford
Pinnacles of Peak History	Clarence Daniels
Saints and Sinners of Ashover	C. E. L. 1924
The Buildings of England (Derbyshire)	Nikolaus Pevsner
The Parish Church of St. Oswald, Ashbourne	(1) F. Jourdain (2) A. E. Sadler
The Cavendish Family	Francis Bickley

For permission to publish illustrative material:

The Vicar, St. Oswalds Church, Ashbourne
The Churchwardens, St. Mary's, Wirksworth
The Vicar and Churchwardens, All Saints, Bakewell
The Parish Priest, St. Michael's R.C. Church, Hathersage
The Vicar, St. John the Baptist, Tideswell
The Vicar, St. Michael and All Angels, Hathersage
The Vicar, St. Peter's Church, Edensor
The Provost, Derby Cathedral

'Wained from the world,
upon it yet I peepe,
Disdaine it weepe for sinne,
and sweetly sleepe'

This book is dedicated to my wife, Denise, for her patience and understanding.

INTRODUCTION

Most Derbyshire churches are post Conquest but often the remains of earlier buildings were indiscriminately incorporated in the structure of their successors. Some places have on display excellent ground plan drawings which should be consulted for architectural references.

The permission of the incumbent must be sought before photographs are taken inside a church or rubbings taken from brasses. In some instances there may be a small charge.

CONTENTS

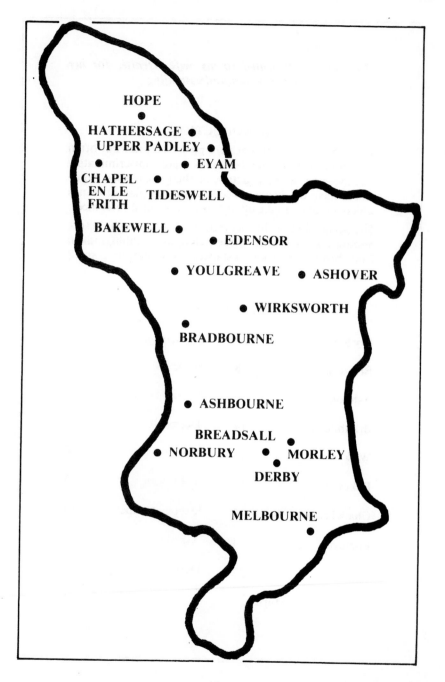

HOPE

HATHERSAGE

UPPER PADLEY

EYAM

CHAPEL
EN LE
FRITH

TIDESWELL

BAKEWELL

EDENSOR

YOULGREAVE

ASHOVER

WIRKSWORTH

BRADBOURNE

ASHBOURNE

BREADSALL

NORBURY

MORLEY

DERBY

MELBOURNE

NORBURY

William the Conqueror granted Norbury Manor to Henry
de Ferrers who gave it to the Monastery of Tutbury. In 1442
Nicholas Fitzherbert did an exchange of lands deal with the
monks and Norbury became his.

Four gargoyles guard the tower and look down on the
toothy crenellations of St. Mary's where ancient archers
sharpened their arrows on the stonework of a south door.
This leads directly to the nave, only three feet longer than the
chancel where most of the builders lie.

The oldest effigy, in stone, is of the fifth Lord Sir Henry
Fitzherbert, a hooded knight in chain armour reposing in the
east chapel of the south aisle. His wife was the daughter of
Ralph Chaddesden and they lived here in the reign of
Edward II.

On the chancel, the single effigy represents Nicholas
(1473) who built the north aisle, the south east chapel, raised
the walls and inserted the clerestory. His armour displays
minute details including a collar with the emblem of Edward
IV. Around the tomb, seventeen figures represent the
children of his two marriages, and the panel at the west end
of the table carries two female figures, perhaps his wives
Alice Bothe and Isabel Ludlow.

Of the children, John, a King's Remembrancer, married a
descendant of Sir William Babington, bought land at Etwall,
started a family line, and had a daughter who married John
Pole of Radbourne and secondly Sir John Port.

Ralph, also armoured, is opposite Nicholas whom he
succeeded, and is with Elizabeth, his wife. He wears the
emblem of Richard III, has his feet on a lion and a tip of his
right foot is supported by a tiny quaint figure of a monk with
a rosary. There is an incised slab of Elizabeth near the tomb
of Nicholas which shows her well wrapped in a winding

cloth, but it is badly mutilated and the inscription is almost unreadable.

Their second son, Henry, a London mercer, married Elizabeth Godwin, daughter of a draper. Thomas, the fourth son, was a rector of Norbury and Precentor of Lichfield, and William, Chancellor of Lichfield. Editha, one of several daughters, married Thomas Babington (considered with Ashover church).

John succeeded, married Benedicta, John Bradbourne's heir, built the church tower planned by his grandfather, added the chapel at the east end, and ended his days a bitter and frustrated man when his only son who married Dorothy Longford, died without an heir. Benedicta produced Anne whose parentage was immediately denied, followed by Jane, admitted to be illegitimate and eventually married off to Anthony Basseford of Bradley Ash. John disowned them all and entailed the estate strictly to his younger brother Anthony.

His will gave detailed instructions for his internment and, exactly where he wanted to be buried, there is a plain large blue marble tomb with alabaster sides and a simple brass plate which tells in Latin that this is where he has lain since 1530.

Anthony, the Recorder of Coventry 1508-1511, was called to the Bar, knighted, became Justice of Common Pleas and one of a delegation of pacification which returned from Ireland to announce that all differences between England and that country would henceforth be settled by arbitration.

When Cardinal Wolsey fell foul of the King, he was lucky to have died in his bed, for Fitzherbert had already prepared a case of treason against him and, when Chancellor Thomas More opposed Henry in the matter of his divorce, he was sent to the block by a Commission which included the Norbury Judge. Shock waves which rippled through the family left him undisturbed for he never allowed sentiment to interfere with the sanctity of the law as he saw it.

His experience persuaded him to compile the *Grande*

Abridgement, the first acceptable codification of English Law and he also translated the Laws of France into English. It is believed he wrote several works on the management and upkeep of manors, including *The Boke of Surveying and Improvements* but, he never attained the highest judicial post of all, the Lord Chief Justice of England.

His memorial on the double brass commemorations (1538) has been damaged but the part to his wife Matilda, heiress of Richard Cotton of Hamstall is intact. She produced five sons and five daughters. Of the girls who are shown on the memorial, two were spinsters, the remainder made good marriages. Son Thomas married Ann Eyre, John took Catherine Fleetwood, Richard married Mary Westcott, and William married Mary, heiress of Humphrey Swinnerton.

Thomas succeeded Sir Anthony, spent more time at Padley than Norbury and died in the Tower in 1591, after twenty years of imprisonment for religious obstinacy for, from the time of Sir Anthony's death, the Catholic element of the family suffered bitterly for its Faith.

Thomas left no heir. His nephew despite being disinherited, succeeded by deceit to Norbury, died without an heir and the manor passed to his brother Anthony. His only son died without issue in 1649, allowing the property to pass to William, grandson of the William who married Mary Swinnerton and great great grandson of Sir Anthony. Thus began the line of Fitzherbert of Swinnerton and Norbury.

These principal family tombs are below the ancient window of the north and south side of the chancel which are presently suffering from age and fungal damage, but the huge east light, recently restored, contains most of the heraldic designs which were in the original work.

Other things of interest in this church are the three piscinas, the 15th century font, a plain bowl mounted on colonades set to form a square, two Saxon cross shafts with intricately carved designs and a good figure of a man and, a superb sensitively carved head of an unknown person on a pillar at the west end.

BREADSALL

This Parish Church was gutted by fire in 1914 when the Suffragettes were alleged to have caused the conflagration which necessitated a complete and careful restoration of the interior.

All Saints which stands proudly above the village owns a tall and slender 14th century spire rising from a thirteenth century tower with stone heads on all sides below the battlements. The stonework is grey and pink and the south door with its niche above is older than the tower of which it is part.

The 1650 Parliamentary Commissioners reported on

'. . . Mr. John Hieron, incumbent, an able preacher, of good conversion . . .'

Mr. Hieron was born in 1608, the son of a Puritan minister from near Burton on Trent. Following an early education at Repton, he studied at Christ College, Cambridge, and after ordination (1633) was appointed to a lectureship in Ashbourne. The onset of the Civil War found him at Derby and then Sir John Gell appointed him to Breadsall where he remained until 1662 when he was ejected for Non Conformity.

Hieron had, according to his writings, an unusual number of lucky escapes which included; being tossed by a cow, falling out of a bedroom window, falling into the Trent and, when alone in a boat being swept away by high winds towards a treacherous whirlpool from which he was rescued at the brink.

He was a sincere and hardworking minister, the author of several theological works including *Sermons for the relief of melancholy Christians* and is recorded as having preached in more than sixty churches in Derbyshire and as

8

many elsewhere. When ejected from Breadsall, he went to live at Little Eaton, moved to Loscoe, died there in 1682 and is buried at Heanor.

Inside All Saints, there is a plain memorial to Erasmus Darwin, who was born in 1731, sent to Chesterfield School at the age of ten, and then to St. John's, Cambridge. In 1754, at Edinburgh he qualified in medicine and set up in practice in Nottingham but as the patients did not come, moved on to Lichfield. There he built a large and lucrative practice and a happy family life with his wife Mary by whom he had three sons. The youngest was the father of Charles Darwin, author of the *Origin of Species.* During this time, George III invited him to become his personal physician, but Darwin refused.

Mary died in 1770 and Anna Seward, the poetess 'Swan of Lichfield' set her cap at him, but he took for his second wife the wealthy widow of Col. Chandos Pole whom he met when attending her children and, even in her husband's life-time, sent her posies of passionate poems.

In Lichfield, Darwin moved in a large circle of influential friends including Josiah Wedgewood, the potter, with whom he cooperated in initiating the Trent and Mersey (Grand Trunk) canal (1766). He corresponded with Priestley and Jacques Rousseau, and though he knew Dr. Johnson and admired his work, disliked him as a man. He founded the Birmingham Lunar Society and set up a botanical garden about which the rejected Anna wrote disparagingly, and with Joseph Wright, William Strutt and others, he created the Derby Philosophical Society.

Poetry flowed readily from his pen, but it was his prose, *Zoomania or the Laws of Organic Life* which created the greatest interest in the scientific circles of the day. This work stimulated his grandson and led him towards his own important contribution to scientific thought which eventually discredited his grandfather's theory.

The second Mrs. Darwin, who gave Erasmus four sons and three daughters, disliked Lichfield, so the family moved to Radbourne Hall and then to Derby, finally settling at Breadsall Priory, where Erasmus died in 1802.

In the church fire of 1914, the font was damaged beyond repair and had to be replaced, but several fragments of charred pages from the Book of Common Prayer and a Bible were rescued after the event and are displayed. Unfortunately, the conflagration destroyed a 15th century screen, restored only seven years earlier. The new one (1929) is the work of H. W. Whitaker, son of the rector, who is commemorated on a small brass. A second miniature brass plate remembers Robert Davison who worked for 14 months on the restoration before being killed in France in 1916, at the age of 22.

The oldest stone carving inside the church is an upside down face just above the piscina on the chancel, and immediately opposite, above the vestry door, one of the new stone corbells represents Joan of Arc, patron of France, a country much in the minds of the British during the work of restoration. In the Lady chapel, in the north aisle, there is an interesting medieval Pieta, found below the floor during the 19th century restoration.

ASHBOURNE

The Parish Church of St. Oswald was dedicated in 1214 by Hugh Pateshull. The slender 214 foot spire was added between 1300 and 1330. A Norman church on this site superseded an earlier Saxon foundation mentioned in the Domesday Book (1086) but there are no easily detected traces of these.

Inside the church, the visitor soon becomes aware of the threads that weave the pattern of history, especially in the north transept where, amongst others, several tombs of the Cockaynes provide, with one exception, a continuous family line, from 1372 to 1592.

Soldiery and Government was the lifestyle of the influential Cockaynes from the 14th century until the reign of Charles II. Edmund died (1403) fighting for the King at

Shrewsbury. Legend suggests that he was brought back here for burial where he lies in effigy alongside his father.

A later Sir Thomas 'The Magnificent', twice County High Sheriff, a 'Noble knight and not a Scholar' fought in the Scottish wars, was knighted on the field at the siege of Tournai (1518) by Henry VIII, upon whom he attended at the Field of the Cloth of Gold in 1520. He died in 1537 and his rhyming epitaph is said to be the oldest in England.

These tombs, in the Boothby Chapel, which also holds tombs of the Bradbourne family, is lit by a window containing 13th century grisaille fragments, some of which came from Fenny Bentley, and all are protected by a medieval oak screen.

At the entrance to the chapel, the marble mural monument of another Sir Thomas Cockayne, grandson of the 'Magnificent' commemorates also his wife and their ten children. This gentleman received the accolade at Edinburgh and like his grandfather, served several terms as High Sheriff. In that capacity he was commanded to 'attend the Queene at Derbie but with a small traine' when Mary, Queen of Scots, was in transit between Wingfield and Tutbury, but his most lasting memory and mark in history was his foundation (1585) of what later became the Ashbourne Grammar School. In the closing years of his life, he completed his *Treatise on Hunting, compiled for the delight of Noblemen and Gentlemen.*

At the dead of night in 1539 Sir Thomas was buried according to family custom and this monument was moved to its present position in the nineteenth century.

The Cockayne fortune, much diminished in the cause of Royalty, ran out in the reign of Charles II when the estate in Ashbourne went to the Boothby family, giving the name to this chapel in which they are principally represented by Penelope, an only child, who died at the age of six. Her tombstone is the most poignant monument here, said to be Thomas Banks' finest work and possibly the inspiration for the 'Sleeping Children' monument in Lichfield. Its triple

The coats of arms which illustrate the upper section are:

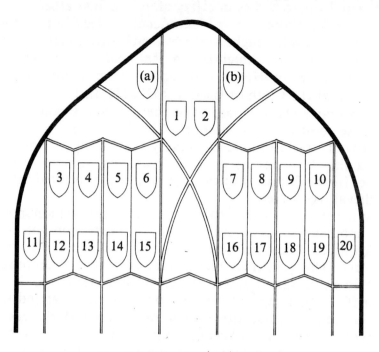

Simplified detail of east window
St. Oswald's Ashbourne

(a)	C. E Kempe the last designer	(b)	An anagram of the initials of Kempe's senior assistant
1	The Duchy of Lancaster	2	John of Gaunt
3	Montgomery	7	Ireland (of Hartshorne)
4	Mackworth	8	de Ferrers
5	Brereton	9	Finderne
6	Lathbury	10	Harthill
11	Corbet	16	Blount
12	Annesley	17	Pole
13	Longford	18	Vernon
14	Franceys (of Foremark)	19	Mynors
15	Hartington	20	Knyveton (Original donors)

inscription extolls her beauty and notes her intelligence. Mrs Delaney, friend of George III, describes Penelope's father, Sir Brooke Boothby, as 'One of those who think themselves pretty gentlemen du premier ordre'. His *Sorrows Sacred to the memory of Penelope* is listed with his literary and political works. He was a devotee of Rousseau, lived temporarily in France, died in Boulogne in 1824, aged 80, and is buried in the family cemetery.

The medieval Knivetons are commemorated by their coat of arms in the great east window, of which they were the original donors. One of them, William de Kniveton, was sentenced to 'six floggings on six consecutive Sundays round Lichfield Cathedral, and as many through the market place on market days' and the Archdeacon of Stafford was required to 'fustigate' once in person, after William had admitted the folly of adultery! Forty years later, in the reign of Richard II, his son Henry, a vicar of Norbury, founded a chantry here.

The glass in the east window is a combination of ancient and modern art and a fund of local information for those interested in heraldry. Most of the arms in the upper section are coeval with the original window but others were added when Charles Kempe re-designed the glasswork in the 19th century. Kempe often gave his angels wings of peacock feathers and the 'eyes' can clearly be seen on the wings of the angels in the lower section.

The Corbet arms is modern and represents the family who were the donors of the renovation. Of the others, Sir Walter Blount (or Blunt) is interesting because he was Royal Standard Bearer to Henry IV, at the battle of Shrewsbury where he met his death acting as a decoy for Henry.

Other coats of arms may be studied here especially on the Cockayne monuments where Edmond is shown wearing his coat of arms as it was intended to be worn, over his armour.

BRADBOURNE

When the Domesday survey was taken (1085-86), Brad-bourne was served by two canons from Dunstable Priory which owned considerable land hereabouts. In 1670, the Parliamentary Commissioners observed that this 'viccarage endowed was really worth fortye pounds per annum' and the vicar 'Mr. Thomas Miles, a man of good repute', an improvement on 1214 when the Priory had a suit in the Court of Rome against William, 'a vicar' who 'kept a concubine and went ahunting, forsaking his tonsure and clerical duties'. After 1300, the canons were replaced by a secular man!

In the Court of Chancery, the people of nearby Atlow disputed a charge for repairs to All Saints when it fell into decay in about 1627. The villagers maintained that their responsibility was only for the upkeep of 'one peece or part of the churchyard wall', of about twenty yards 'called by the name of the Atlow part'. They lost their case.

The reliable solidity of the remaining Norman tower gives some idea of how substantial the original foundation must have been. The decorated doorway on the outer south side of the tower and the large arch inside are both Norman. The remainder of the building is of various later dates.

The square font, of uncertain age but probably pre-1280, is of particular interest, because of its comparative rarity and size. It is taken from a solid block of stone 2½ feet square, lined with lead, and decorated with a simple quatrefoil pattern and, unexpectedly on the north wall of this English village church, a 17th century Italian painting contrasts vividly with the cruder native wall painting of about the same date opposite.

In the churchyard, there is a repaired Saxon Cross with a vicissitudinous history. It was reported standing in 1816. In 1833, Glover discovered it being used for a gate-post, and J. C. Cox in 1867 waxed about its 'fast perishing through friction incidental to its utilitarian position' — as a stile!

WIRKSWORTH

The church of St. Mary the Virgin is one of the most interesting buildings in the County. It is perhaps the oldest Christian foundation of ancient Mercia after Repton from where Abbess Eadburger sent a coffin made of Wirksworth lead for the burial of St. Guthlac of Croyland in 714.

Dating from 1270, St. Mary's followed a Norman building on the site of an earlier Saxon one. It contains from some time between those two periods a remarkable, probably unique, carved stone incorporated in the fabric of the north wall. Discovered in 1820-21 in front of the altar lying two feet below ground level, overturned and covering a vault which contained a complete human skeleton; the reason for its reversal was then and is now, a mystery. Suggestions are that the Normans, anxious to eradicate all native culture, may have overturned it, or that it was the work of Cromwell's men who are also alleged to have ejected the huge Norman font which now stands in the north transept. The stone, measuring 5 feet by 2 feet 10 inches, is considered to be the cover of a sarcophagus probably belonging to an early priest, perhaps the founder of this ancient mission, reputedly one named Betti of whom little is known, except that he came into this part of the country with two other priests who are accounted for, with Paeda, a Christian princess from Northumbria. The stonemason's message, understood to be eight scenes from the life of Christ, makes a visit to St. Mary's worthwhile.

On the north side of the chancel are all that are left of the tombs of the Gell family. The oldest is inscribed with the figure of Ralph (1564), his wives Godeth and Emma. Their four sons and ten daughters are neatly represented around the sides of the table. Lying next to them is a very fine monument to Anthony, their eldest son. A tablet nearby tells that he was 'one of the worshipfull companie of the Bench of the Inner Temple in London' . . . and 'He, at his only cost and charges, founded the Free Grammar Schoole and Almshouses in the town of Wirksworthe'.

The Grammar School, now used by a furniture restorer, was rebuilt in 19th century Gothic style, complete with crocketed pinnacles. It stands north east of the church and is adjacent to the Almshouses.

Anthony was the uncle of John Gell, member of Parliament and High Sheriff in 1635. His duties then included the levying of ship money about which he quarrelled with Sir John Stanhope of Elvaston, subsequently summoned by the Council for refusing the Sheriff's demand. Gell construed Stanhope's stubborness as a personal insult. When Stanhope died, Gell went into the church, defaced his monument and wooed the widow who became his second wife. Gell pursued her — or so detractors said — 'for nothing else but to destroy the glory of her husband and his house'.

Gell was created Baronet in 1642 when he raised a regiment of foot described by Mrs. Hutchins as ' . . . good stout fighting men but the most licentious that belonged to the Parliament' and by Derby citizens as ' . . robbers and plunderers'.

He was condemned and sent to the Tower in 1650 for plotting against the Commonwealth but was pardoned in 1653. When he died in London in 1671 his body was brought to Wirksworth on a cart. The journey took six weeks and along the route crowds gathered to view the passing cortege.

Opposite, the effigy of the knight is to Anthony Lowe (1599) who married Bridget, daughter of Sir John Fogge of Kent. Anthony was standard bearer to Henry VIII, Edward VI, and Queen Mary, and a Gentleman of the Bedchamber. He was granted by Henry VIII, in 1528, from the Duchy of Lancaster, the manor of Alderwasley which remained with the family until the marriage of Elizabeth, fifth in descent from Anthony, to Nicholas Hurt. Pevsner considers this Renaissance style monument the best in the church.

There are also stone carvings of uncertain age, origin and

Lead miner with Pick and Kibble

meaning, dotted around here, especially at the north door. The Queen of Hearts, fragments of scroll work, knots and animal heads, and in the s. transept an interesting little figure known as the Wirksworth Lead Miner brought here from nearby Bonsall! A little south of the sarcophagus cover already mentioned, and above the glass case containing a copy of the *Breeches Bible,* there is a carving of Adam and the serpent in the Garden of Eden.

Local history is enhanced by many wall tablets in this church, such as that of the Rev. Abraham Benet, F.R.S., curate here for twenty three years, and later rector of Fenny Bentley. Besides being a chaplain to the Duke of Devonshire and librarian to the Duke of Bedford, he was the author of *New experiments in Electricity* which, says the plaque 'established his reputation for science'. He died in 1859. Outside, a plaque recalls Philip Shallcross 'eminent quill driver to the attorneys of this town . . . ' who had 'an invincible attachment to dogs and cats'.

(Photograph: the author)

In the churchyard, with the stump of an ancient cross, there are stone coffins and somewhere, in an unmarked grave, the remains of Elizabeth Evans, Methodist worker and wife of Samuel, a local preacher. George Eliot, reputedly based Dinah Morris, the character in Adam Bede, on her aunt Elizabeth Evans.

17

BAKEWELL

The skeleton of a young girl was found in one of the stone coffins which stand beside the outer west wall of All Saints, and another contained a chalice belonging to an ancient priest. They were recovered in the 19th century along with one of the finest collections of inscribed coffin lids in England which are now principally displayed in the south porch. The most recent discovery, a 12th century headstone came to light during some work in 1959 and this is in the church.

Further evidence of a very early Christian settlement can be deduced from the remains of the stone crosses which are showing signs of weathering and neglect.

King John presented this church and its chapelries to the Dean and Chapter of Lichfield in the 1100's but it was mentioned in the Saxon Chronicles (940) and the Domesday Survey in 1086 when it shared with Repton alone in Derbyshire the distinction of having two priests.

Of the several interesting features of this church, few attract more attention than the Vernon Chapel which houses the tombs and monuments of that family who did not have a right of internment at Haddon. Romantic tales woven around the names of Dorothy Vernon and John Manners are baseless but it is a fact that their marriage united both their names and the lands which are now the property of the Dukes of Rutland.

Richard de Redvers, Lord of Vernon, arrived with the Conqueror. His great great grandson Richard de Vernon married Alice, daughter and co-heiress of William Avenell who held, with other estates, the lands of Haddon which eventually passed to Richard, who settled there.

The Manners, who also came in 1066, were prominent courtiers, especially in Tudor times.

Thomas, son of George Manners and Anne, the daughter of Sir Thomas Leger, was a favourite of Henry VIII, whom he attended on the Field of the Cloth of Gold (1520) and at the meeting between Henry and Charles of France. A year later, he was appointed Royal Cupbearer and the following year received the Stewardship of Pickering in Yorkshire, to which the Wardenship of Sherwood Forest was added in 1541. Dubbed Knight of the Garter in 1525, he was then elevated to the Earldom of Rutland. He was at the Coronation of King Henry and Ann Boleyn, and later participated in the trial which led to that Queen's execution. In 1542, he was appointed Lord Chamberlain to Anne of Cleves and Constable of Nottingham Castle.

Thomas fathered eleven children of whom the eldest, Henry, succeeded to the title in 1543. Except for one short lapse in the reign of Mary, he remained at Court, a favourite to the end.

The memorial to Dorothy (1584), her husband Sir John Manners (1611) and four children provides an essential bridge across history.

Dorothy was the daughter of Sir George Vernon by his first wife Margaret. His lavish lifestyle brought him the nickname of 'King of the Peak'. He died on the 9th August 1567 and lies between two wives — carved in alabaster, bearded and quite sumptuous — his wives plain and alike. The absence of dates on a tomb usually suggests it was made before the recipients died.

Opposite the memorial of John and Dorothy, there is a pretentious monument to George, their eldest son who married Grace Pierrepoint, principally remembered for her foundation of the Lady Manners' Grammar School. Nine children are commemorated on this disproportionate affair. Each has been allocated a strident biblical text which, with other quotations, make it all rather overwhelming.

During the 19th century restoration, workmen who exposed the bones of Dorothy Vernon found hair still on the skull, and a report of 1841 noted that a second skull, possibly belonging to Grace Pierrepoint, had been inexpertly opened.

The remains of Sir John Wednesley (or Wensley) were also

moved. He used the power of a medieval landlord in a crude way when he broke into the home of a Geoffrey Rowland, held him prisoner for six days and then chopped off his right hand. Sir John was killed fighting on the Lancastrian side at the battle of Shrewsbury (1403). His damaged tomb is here probably because of a connection with the Guild of the Holy Cross and the chantry founded by Sir Godfrey and Lady Ann Foljambe, in 1344.

There is only one memorial to the Foljambes here today, but we may presume that others have been lost in the upheavals of various restorations.

The Foljambes were the Lords of numerous manors, and the Steward of John of Gaunt, Duke of Lancaster. A monument 20 inches by about 27, with waist length figures only 12 inches tall, exquisitely worked in alabaster, is described by Pevsner as 'internationally remarkable'. It shows Sir Geoffrey in mail armour and his second wife Avena with an elaborate and lovely head-dress. Sir Geoffrey was 59 when he died but Avena, daughter of Sir Thomas Ireland, survived him and remarried.

Foljambe memorial

(Photograph: the author)

A large mural in the body of the church is Matthew Strutt's, a 'well known and respected farrier and vet' who had 'zeal for the house of God and unremitting attention to the airy business of the belfry. He caught a cold which terminated his existence May 25th 1798, in the 68th year of his age!'

In the graveyard, gravestones tell the sad tale of infant and child mortality. Although Robert Bradbury managed to survive to the age of 74, in 1792, he is remembered here with three children who died in infancy, and the remaining six before the age of nine. Then the Winson family, between 1839 and 1855, lost six children, the youngest at only 10 months, the longest survivor at the age of five.

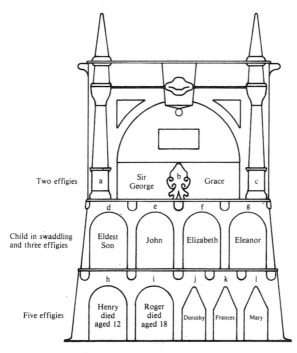

Outline of monument to Sir George Manners, his wife and their several children.

The biblical quotations included on the monument are as follows:
a. Christ to me both in death and life is an advantage
b. Prayers and thine alms are gone up before God
c. I shall goe to him Hee shall not returne to mee
d. Mine age is nothing in respect of thee
e. One generation passeth and another cometh
f. A vertuos woman is a crown to her husband
g. The wise woman buildeth her house
h. My dayes were but a span long
i. By the grace of God I am what I am
j. A gracious woman retaineth honour
k. A prudent wife is from the Lord
l. Shee that feareth the Lord shall be praysed

Roger Manners is interred at Lincolns Inn, London

CHAPEL EN LE FRITH

This is the only church in the county dedicated to St. Thomas á Becket. The first chapel in the Royal Forest, or Frith, was built around 1225 by the keepers of the Royal Deer. From the outset, they jealously guarded their authority, maintaining it had been granted to them in the days of Alexander, Bishop of Coventry (1224-1228).

The 'Chapel' was enlarged in the 1380's, but by the mid 18th century the outer walls and tower began to deteriorate and were all, except the north side, rebuilt in the present Georgian style. There is a further extension dating from 1975. The interior, built of local pink sandstone, retains most of its 14th century character and just above the graceful and wide chancel arch, there is a tie beam which dates the wooden roof at 1599.

In the north aisle, a mural monument recalls William Bagshaw who in his will, on 15th October 1701, indicated he did not wish to be 'admitted into a place style consecrated' but the 'Apostle of the Peak' is not only buried here — his coat of arms is prominently placed below the monument. Born at Litton and ordained at Chesterfield in 1651, William ministered in Glossop for eleven years before his Nonconformity caused his ejection. He continued to preach despite warrants being issued against him until a month before he died. In 1696, his brother was High Sheriff which is perhaps the reason he was brought to the church.

St. Thomas á Becket's was dreadfully used in 1648 when King Charles' Scottish supporters defeated by Cromwell were brought to the town and —

'1500 put into ye church Sept. 14. They went away Sept. 30 following. They were buried of them before the rest went 44 persons, and more buried Oct. 2 who were not able to march, and the same yet died by the way before they came to Cheshire 10 and more'.

This awful incident brought the town the nickname of 'Derbyshire's Black Hole'.

Another entry in the church records relates how in 1701

> '. . . The great bell in our steeple was taken to be cast upon Friday 27 June, and as it was coming down the pulleys and the bell fell to the ground and brought all before it. The man who was above to guide it was one Ezekiel Shuttleworth, a joyner of this town, he seeing the pulleys break could noways help himself but came after it, a ladder with himself and a little crow of iron in his hand, and yet by God's great preservation had little or no harm . . .'

Mural monuments in the chancel tell of Rev. Hall and Rev. Grundy, two priests who served just short of a century between them, and nearby another, particularly poignant, by the widow of 'Henry Kirk, killed in a shooting accident'.

The enormous box pews installed in 1830, are inscribed on the north side facing the font with the names of all Chaplains and Ministers here since 1339 whilst those on the south side immediately inside the door record from 1631 to 1951, thirteen male members of the Bramwell family, sextons here continually for 300 years.

The 15th century octagonal font is now enclosed by what was a communion rail, carved and initialled by Mr. White, the priest here in 1681. Unfortunately he lost his senses and was pensioned off in 1697 at 4 shillings (20 new pence) a week.

Outside there are several items of interest. The remains of an ancient cross which had been built into a farmhouse wall marks the grave of the farmer to whom the house belonged, and at the eastern end of the graveyard, still in its original place, a 13th century carved stone marks the grave of a forester. Several gravestones round about bear interesting epitaphs.

EDENSOR

Two county churches rebuilt at a stroke are at Foremark and Edensor. Francis Burdett, in 1662, undertook the new work at Foremark where St. Saviour with its Gothic exterior contains elements from the earlier chapelries of Foremark and Ingleby. Workmanship from a previous Norman church of St. Peter was incorporated by Sir Gilbert Scott when he rebuilt Edensor in 1867. Similarity ends there. The former was rebuilt when an earlier foundation fell into decay, whilst St. Peter's was re-located with the village when the sixth Duke of Devonshire planned an unobstructed view from Chatsworth.

Except the south doorway, with its flat faced gargoyle, all the transferred stonework is inside the church. There are no early monuments, but at the rebuilding the enormous affair in the east end was brought in. This commemorates Henry (1616) and William (1625), first and second sons of Sir William Cavendish of Chatsworth, Treasurer of the Chamber, Privy Counsellor to Henry VIII, Edward VI, and Queen Mary. He married Elizabeth, relict of Robert Barley who being the daughter of John Hardwick, is best known as 'Bess of Hardwick'.

The sons are in effigy, Henry, a skeleton on a straw mat,

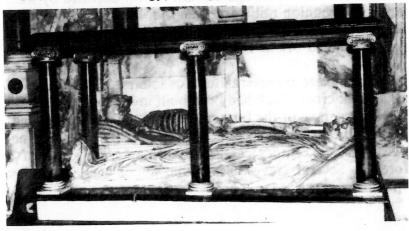

(Photograph: the author)

24

and William, enshrouded up to his neck, lying top to tail with his brother in what looks like a four poster bed of marble, actually an altar tomb in front of what was the reredos in the old church. It has Fame with her trumpet flanked on either side by huge tablets bearing epitaphs in Latin, and alcoves with the sculptured robes and coronet of William, and military accoutrements of Henry. He made a slight name for himself during wars in the low countries and represented Derby in six Parliaments, although his restless nature and preference for travel precluded his taking too close an interest in political affairs. Grace, the eldest daughter of his stepfather became his wife, through the insistence of his mother with whom he did not get on. He sold his inheritance to his brother, but retained property at Tutbury as dower for his wife by whom he had no issue, and bequeathed Doveridge and Church Broughton to his four illegitimate sons.

His brother, educated with the children of Talbot, sixth Earl of Shrewsbury whom his mother married, was M.P. for Liverpool in 1586, represented Newport in 1588, and became High Sheriff of this county in 1595. When Princess Sophia, who lived only for one day, was christened in 1605, he was created Baron Chatsworth of Hardwick. His epitaph describes him as 'A man to execute every laudable enterprise, and in the simplicity of virtue, rather deserving than courting Glory'. Thus he attended King James on a progress in 1618, and in that year was made Earl of Devonshire and Hardwick, for which honour he was said to have paid £10,000.

Ann, daughter of Henry Keighley, was his wife, followed by Elizabeth, daughter of Sir Edward Boughton, widow of Sir Richard Wortley. By her, he had John who died a year before his father was made Lord Lieutenent of the County, in 1619.

This dual monument is simply described by Cox as:

    ' . . a good specimen of the costly but heathenish
    art of England's great men'.

An altogether more discreet tablet records Lord Frederick, son of the seventh Duke of Devonshire

'. . . sent out as Chief Secretary for Ireland and murdered within twelve hours of landing, at Phoenix Park, Dublin, May 6th 1882, aged 45 . . '

made more poignant by the wreath of everlasting flowers, final tribute of Queen Victoria, perserved in a case nearby. The Duke is interred in the graveyard where 300 M.P.s attended his funeral with a crowd of 30,000 other people.

The village of Edensor was designed by Sir Joseph Paxton, architect, landscape gardener, member of Parliament for Coventry, and friend of the sixth Earl. He also re-shaped the gardens at Chatsworth where his enormous greenhouse became the model for the Great Hall (Crystal Palace) at the London Exhibition of 1851. Sir Joseph rose from humble stock, married Sarah Bown of Matlock and, died on the 8th June 1865, at Sydenham. He is commemorated on an enamelled plaque at the back of this church.

At the extreme edge of the graveyard, beyond the south door, an incised slab before a simple gravestone, marks the spot where President John F. Kennedy stood on the 29th June 1963, when he visited the grave of his sister.

'. . . Kathleen 1920-48, widow of Major, the Marquis of Hartington, killed in action, and daughter of Joseph Kennedy, sometime Ambassador of the United States to Great Britain'.

(Photograph: the author)

26

EYAM

The story of Eyam, Derbyshire's Plague Village, is so well annotated it is uneccessary to offer more than a reminder of those grim days in 1665-66 when the village population was sadly reduced by the Great Plague, said to have arrived here in a bale of infected second hand clothing from London.

But for the vicar, William Mompesson, and Thomas Stanley, the ejected Nonconformist he replaced, the disease might have spread further afield. Rector Mompesson sent his children out of the village when the epidemic was recognised but his twenty seven year old wife chose to remain. She fell victim to the disease on 26th August 1666. Catherine, who came here from County Durham, has a large tomb beside the cross in the graveyard. Thomas Stanley died four years later and is commemorated in this church dedicated to St. Lawrence.

It seems probable that Eyam's first church was built about the time of Henry I. It is not mentioned in the Domesday Book but was valued in the Taxation Rolls of Pope Nicholas IV in 1291. Its early history gives another interesting insight to changing family fortunes, manorial rights and patronage.

Roger Monteyne, whose principal seat was at Risley, sold the advowson of the church to Thomas Furnival in 1307. The fourth and last Baron Furnival died in 1383. By his wife Thomasia he had a daughter Joan who brought the estates to Thomas Neville who took, through his wife, the title of Lord Furnival and appeared in Parliament under that name. Joan died in 1395 and what is believed to be her effigy is in St. James' Church, Barlbrough. This marriage produced a daughter Maud, who became the wife of John Talbot, first Earl of Shrewsbury, 'The Scourge of France' who died at Chatillon, in 1435. His sixth successor became the husband of Bess of Hardwick through whom these lands passed to various branches of her family. They still hold the advowson of the church.

Anna Seward, the 'Swan of Lichfield' and devotee of

Dr. Darwin, was born here in 1747. Her father was rector before he moved to Lichfield when Anna was seven years of age. In this rectory, before she could read, she could recite *L'Allegro* and *Il Penseroso,* and by her ninth year could recall from memory the first three books of *Paradise Lost.* Her portrait was painted by George Romney and in her will she bequeathed her poems to Sir Walter Scott who published them in 1810.

The very fine cross described in 1818 was 'according to village tradition, found on the neighbouring hills . . . is curiously ornamented and embossed with a variety of figures and designs characterised by different symbolic devices . . .'

About a century before that was written, an extraordinary event took place in the local pub when the rector, something the worse for his addiction to the bottle, in a mock ceremony married the landlord's daughter. News of this reached the Bishop who obliged John Hunt to legally marry the girl. Hunt was subsequently sued for breach of promise. Litigation cost him most of his fortune and many friends. He died in the rectory and was buried on 16th December 1709, six years after his wife Anna.

Many objects of interest in this church include the early font, wall murals discovered only twenty years ago, and outside around the walls below the ancient sundial, a number of incised grave slabs.

HATHERSAGE

This mainly 14th century church is another legacy of Victorian restoration for before the arrival of Rev. H. Cottingham, in 1851, it was described as ' . . . in the most despicable order', but now evidence of the care lavished on St. Michael's is everywhere.

The most notable remembrances are to the Eyre family who probably came to England with the Conqueror and held land at Hope before Nicholas Eyre fought at Agincourt. They established a foothold at Hathersage in the 1400's, when Robert, descendant of Nicholas Eyre, married Joan the heiress of Robert of Padley whose manor was in this parish. They largely rebuilt this church.

Their crest is below the battlements which crown the porch, and on the font with that of Padley, indicating a joint family donation. Interesting brasses commemorate the union of Robert and Joan which produced eleven sons and four daughters. Of the sons, three died without issue; the remainder, by careful and judicious marriages, strenghtened the hand of Eyre over Newbold, Hassop and Highlow from whence came Robert, High Sheriff in 1638. Others went further afield.

Ann, the surviving child of Sir Arthur Eyre, and great great granddaughter of Robert and Joan, married Sir Thomas Fitzherbert.

St. Michael's offers excellent facilities for brass rubbing enthusiasts.

Other monuments which deserve notice are to the ship-building Cammel family, one of whom died in America 'from the result of a fall, in 1891'. Another records Reverend James Cutler, vicar here for 45 years, just short of the record of John Le Cornn of St. Ouen, Jersey, who served for 50 years, and in the Lady Chapel, there are memorials to the influential Shuttleworth family.

The large 'Kempe' window overlooking the high altar came from the church in Derwent village submerged by the flooding of the Ladybower Reservoir (1945) and the ancient parish chest required to have three keys stands near the font. Besides the Lady Chapel is a strange memento, the chairs used by Queen Victoria and Prince Albert at the opening of St. George's Hall, Liverpool, built of Hathersage stone.

What legend says is the grave of Little John, companion of Robin Hood, is maintained here by the Ancient Order of Foresters. When a more recent grave was being dug, on 31st May 1781, the corpse of Benjamin Ashton, buried fifty six years previously, was discovered congealed 'hard as flint'. Benjamin was 'reared upright in the church' whilst awaiting

Chairs used by Queen Victoria and Prince Albert at the opening of St. George's Hall, Liverpool, built of Hathersage stone.

(Photograph: the author)

re-interment but he fell over and his head dropped off. A man named Sherd attempted to saw off a piece as a souvenir, but found his implement inadequate for the task.

Finally, it should not be forgotten that Charlotte Bronte, an occasional visitor to Hathersage, based Morton in her novel *Jane Eyre* on this place.

HOPE

It is more likely that an ancient Saxon church with its own priest stood on this site of St. Peter's. Then the priest also held a carucate of land. ˙

By the time of Bishop Alexander Savensby (1224-1238) it had become an important parish church where the priest received the Easter dues, all oblations, mortuary, marriage and purification fees, special fees collected on certain days of the year, as well as tithes on pigs, poultry and calves.

This brought a sizeable income of about £9.50 a year which, when the Valor Ecclesiasticus was compiled in the reign of Henry VIII, had been increased by further tithes of corn, hay and minerals. Then the rectory, together with its glebe and lands was also assessed at a little over £5.00.

St. Peter's spire of early date rises directly from the tower.

This tends to emphasize its squatness giving the appearance of a short fat cigar. The building is battlemented all around and there are gargoyles of many shapes and sorts.

Inside, a huge and plain circular font stands on an octagonal base and nearby, two full sized foliated slabs with designs clearly indicating that they were once on the grave of Royal Forest officials. On the chancel, the sedilia is graduated in the usual manner and there is also a piscina with a single pointed arch.

The east window holds the corn sheaf insignia of Kempe and, in the south asle, another by the same artist shows clearly his use of peacock 'eyes' on the angel wings. Before it was restored, this window contained the Gell coat of arms, probably inserted in the reign of Edward VI, (1547-53) when Ralph Gell held the lease of Hope Manor. Ralph, who died in 1564, was the grandfather of Sir John Gell, the celebrated Parliamentary General remembered at Wirksworth.

The only early glass here is a small panel in the Lady Chapel window where the ancient arms of the Eyres have been inserted.

Visitors to St. Peter's cannot help but be impressed by the extraordinary number of carvings and initials which seem to be everywhere. In the choir and chancel, the black oak panelling is carved with arms of the local Eyres and Reresby's, who have family connections with the Sitwells and the Sacheverells. These examples of the woodcarvers' skill are the backs of early box pews and are variously dated 1587 to 1690. Also on the north wall of the choir, a set of initials confirms an ownership, and the skillfully carved pulpit advertises:

> 'Thos Bocking, teacher, the Churchwardens
> this year Michael Woodhead, Jarvis Hallam,
> John Haye 1652'.

The single complete brass here, quite unlike any other mentioned in this booklet, is only 9 inches by 12 inches, to Henry Balguy. It is quaint rather than beautiful and shows an extraordinary image of Henry in his doublet, breeches and pointed headgear, a pen in one hand and a book in the other. The whole is surprisingly amateurish and even the inscription is oddly done. A translation reads:

'Wained from the world, upon it yet I peepe,
Disdaine it weepe for sinne, and sweetly sleepe'.

Odd though this may seem, it is important and was probably completed before Henry's death, to his own design. It shows us how he saw himself, an elegant gentleman and scholar. He was from a family of wealthy landowners with extensive estates at Aston, the principal family seat, and Derwent Hall, near Hathersage, now lost under the Ladybower Reservoir.

On the north side of the church there are several named pews, including one to 'Henry Balguy, 1652' and more initials are cut into the paving of the aisles and around the font, behind which two boards give details of charitable bequests. A third tells us: 'This chancel was beautifyed in 1730'. The 'beautifying' included whitewashing and plastering (since removed) which Dr. Cox angrily describes as a 'barbarity'. We may wonder how he would have reacted in 1970-74 when the building was re-roofed with stainless steel!.

In the churchyard, there is what remains of a very early cross, rediscovered in the 1850's when the village school into which it had been built was demolished and, over the doorway of the south porch, a small niche contains a statue of St. Peter. In the 19th century, when foxes ravaged livestock, the churchwardens paid a fee for dead foxes delivered to them. Then the corpses were exhibited in this niche as proof of legitimate expenditure.

A strange ceremony took place in the churchyard in the last quarter of the 18th century when the remains of a grazier and his maid servant were brought down from the moors where they had been for almost half a century. The unfortunate pair were lost in a snow storm and covered over from

January until the following May, by which time their corpses were so offensive, the coroner ordered immediate burial.

Some twenty years later, the graves were reopened and it was found that the bodies had not deteriorated further. For the next several years, they were opened each summer for the satisfaction of morbid public interest until the dead man's grandson put a stop to the gruesome business by insisting on a decent final burial, in the churchyard.

UPPER PADLEY CHAPEL

Upper Padley, one of the most tranquil parts of Derbyshire, came into the possession of the Eyre family at the beginning of the 15th century when the devout and influential Roman Catholic Robert Eyre, of Hathersage, married Joan Padley. Four generations later, Anne Eyre, heiress and only survivor of her parents married Sir Thomas, son and heir of the celebrated judge Fitzherbert of Norbury. Thomas died in the Tower (1591) where he was imprisoned for 20 years for consistently refusing to give up his Catholic faith.

George Talbot, sixth Earl of Shrewsbury and Lord Lieutenant of Derbyshire, was a calculating and ruthless hunter of Catholics in the county and the Padley family were particularly harrassed for their stubborness. In 1587, Talbot's agent John Manners reported that he went with Roger Columbell and a group of men to Padley to search out John Fitzherbert, son of Thomas and Ann, but he wasn't there.

Twelve months later, Padley Hall was raided again, this time under the command of Talbot in person. Two Catholic priests were arrested together with John Fitzherbert and taken to Derby Gaol to await the Summer Assizes.

One of the priests, Nicholas Garlick, came from a respected Glossop family. He served as a schoolteacher at Tideswell before entering the English College at Rheims in

Padley Chapel, (near Grindleford).

1582 and following his ordination a year later returned to England — only to be expelled in 1585. He returned again from Europe a year later to continue his missionary work.

More than likely Garlick knew Robert Ludlam who came from Sheffield. He was also ordained at Rheims and returned to England in 1582.

In prison, they met Richard Sympson who had been tried earlier but embraced Protestantism for the price of his life. The Padley men persuaded him to recant. The result was that all three priests were found guilty and condemned to die a barbarous death on July 23rd 1588.

The sentence read:

> 'That you and each of you be carried to the place from whence you came, and thence be drawn on a hurdle to the place of execution, and there be severally hanged, but cut down while you are alive; that your privy members be cut off; that your bowels be taken out and burned before your faces; that your heads be severed from your bodies; that your bodies be divided into four quarters, and that your quarters be at the Queen's disposal; and the Lord have mercy on your souls'.

An eye witness said they went to their death 'without the least sign of fear or dismay', but Garlick had noticed that Sympson seemed frightened and so took his place first at the scaffold. He had to wait there whilst the cauldron which would receive his hacked body was brought to the boil. Meanwhile, he calmly addressed the crowd of assembled spectators. Robert Ludlam, when he climbed the scaffold, raised his eyes in prayer and called out 'Venite Benedicti Dei' (Come you blessed of God) just as he was flung off the ladder to the jerk of the hangman's noose.

The heads and quartered bodies of the three men were set up on poles on St. Mary's Bridge, Derby, but with the connivance of a watchman, were secretly taken down by a group of Catholic men who buried them at night with as much decency as possible.

Thomas, son of John Fitzherbert of Norbury and nephew of Thomas of Padley who disinherited him, obtained both Norbury and Padley by trickery when his uncle's will was destroyed by Richard Topcliffe on the advice of Bishop Whitcliffe. Later it was alleged that young Thomas had made an arrangement with Topcliffe, the torturer, to destroy certain members of the Fitzherbert family and when Thomas claimed that Topcliffe had not kept his part of the bargain, he was sued for £5,000. In the course of the trial into this 'delicate matter', Topcliffe was imprisoned for uttering unseemly remarks about the privy council, but on release became the owner of Padley, where he lived from 1603 to 1604. When he died he left the property to his daughter.

There is nothing left today of Padley Hall, once one of the grandest in this part of the county, except some of the foundations which have been arranged to form an outdoor amphitheatre for the reception and assembly of pilgrims. The domestic chapel which adjoined the Hall, and is not much changed architecturally, has survived. It was used as a cow byre and hay shed when Cox wrote of it in the 1870's but when the altar stone was found in 1933 it was restored as a chapel for the use of Roman Catholics. The renewed windows show the arrest of the priests and representations of St. Mary's Bridge in Derby. The chapel may be reached by footpath which starts at Grindleford station and leads into National Trust Property.

TIDESWELL

This magnificent building stretching over 50 yards from east to west, and 26 yards from north to south, is worthy of its epithet 'Cathedral of the Peak'. Its tall tower with a little room over the porch, dominates this small town which has had a church since earliest times.

Cox praises the . . . 'delicacy of . . . mouldings . . . the effective character of the buttresses . . . grace of tracery and proportion of the component parts . . . which . . . all combine in the production of a building . . . it would be no easy task to equal by any of like size in the Kingdom'. Yet, a century before, Dr. Pegge complained of 'a beautiful building that will speedily be in a ruinous condition if not repaired . . .' and Mary Sterndale, a contemporary of Cox remarked that the . . . 'ancient font . . . is now regularly used by work-people to mix their colours in when they "beautifyed" the church with blue and mahogany paint . . .'

On the chancel, there is a brass to Canon Andrew (1864-1900) who masterminded a 19th century restoration, including the exceptionally detailed and beautifully carved modern oak choir stalls created by craftsmen from Sussex. Those they replaced are now in the chapel of the north transept. Thus 'Victorian Restorers' more often than not maligned, have left this County indebted to their foresight.

In 1254, (although the foundation is earlier), the vicar here had a good living. Apart from the usual altar fees and tithes, there were others from two mills, Peter's pence (a special collection) plough fees of a half penny for each, and more on hemp, flax, vegetables and honey. An income came from a chantry founded by John Fulljambe (John Foljambe) by licence of Edward III, and pre-Reformation Robert Bayley gave land on condition of a payment of '2 shillings a year for prayers at the altar of the Blessed Mary . . .'.

There are many monuments of great interest in St. John the Baptist's Church, the oldest being the ladies whose effigies lie in the north transept. There is no certainty as to who they were but the bold elementary workmanship is probably not later than the 14th century when an earlier church stood on this site. The Foljambes were probably buried there, for John Foljambe (1249) demanded to be buried in the chancel of the church 'with his forefathers'. There were once several monuments to this family but the only one remaining is to John Foljambe (d.1358) who has a brass memorial in the north aisle of the chancel. The original metal, which was probably stolen, was replaced about 1875 by a descendent of the family.

Near to this knight in armour, in the centre of the chancel, an enormous and unusual altar tomb commemorates Sir Simpson Meverell, Constable of England. The sides are in open worked alabaster (recent) and disclose below the slab a wasted corpse wrapped in a kind of winding cloth. The slab which includes five crosses of consecration denoting that it was used as an altar, has a number of elaborate brasses representing, at each corner, an evangelist, with a dedication. These are of a different period to the centre piece representing God the Father who has before Him, resting on an orb, a crucifix with the figure of the Son and a dove, symbolizing the Holy Spirit. The whole is surrounded by a Latin inscription.

The Meverells first came to Tideswell when Thomas of Throwley in Staffordshire married Elizabeth Daniels. Sampson of the monument is their grandson eventually married to Elizabeth, daughter of Sir Roger Leche.

Above all else, Meverell was a fighting man. He served under the Earl of Salisbury, who appointed him to several important posts in France, and later under the Duke of Bedford, uncle of Henry II, and Regent of France. Meverell was knighted at St. Luce, and made King's Constable of

England, fought with the army of Henry V, at Agincourt (1415) and has the distinction of having fought eleven battles in France, mostly instigated by Joan of Arc around Orleans, between 1429 and 1431. In service with John Stafford Archbishop of Canterbury (1443-52), Meverell's life ended when he 'departed from wordly service . . . the which divided his soul from his body MCCCCLXII (1462)'.

This 'knight' was another of what many of his contemporaries were, rough, tough and disputatious. Once he gathered around him a gang of ruffians who terrified jurors called to settle a land dispute. They failed to appear in court to Meverell's advantage!

A second alabaster tomb, in the south transept, also restored in the last century, is, according to the inscription, that of Sir Thurston de Bower and the Lady Margaret, his wife, both living in the reign of Richard II. The effigies, both rather knocked about, are of a knight in armour and a lady, but the de Bowers were yeoman, so the figures on the monument must represent somebody else. Not a lot is known about the de Bowers except that they once held the manor and land of Little Longstone.

In the south aisle, near the entrance to the chapel, is a simple but good brass monument to Robert (1483) and Isabell (1458) Lytton. Robert was Under Treasurer of England in the reign of Henry VI. They retained ownership of Lytton until it was sold in 1597 to John Alsop. The brass, which is in good condition, shows the Chancellor in a long civilian robe with wide sleeves trimmed with ermine. Isabella wears an interesting headdress which became a popular style in the 16th century, and a long high-waisted gown with narrow fur trimmed sleeves. The slab on which the brasses are set seals a tomb where in the 1800's were discovered coffins made of lead.

High on the north wall at the foot of this brass, a mural monument reminds us that Thomas Stathum married ' . . . three wives, Barbara daughter of Cromwell Meverell of Tideswell, near kinsman of Thomas Cromwell, Earl of

Ardglass lineally descended from Frances Meverell of Throwley . . . (and) Mary, relict of Nicholas Shirtcliffe M.D.' The third wife's name is not mentioned but the monument announces that Stathum raised at his own expense a troop of horses for '. . . royal Charles I'. This Stathum was fourth in descent from Sampson Meverell. The family vault below the mural is said to have contained his

> 'tinned coffin, the which he had by him for many years. It had thirty six locks upon it, all locked with one key, which, according to his request, was cast away after his internment'.

Tideswell's 'Vicar of Bray' was the colourful Robert Pursglove, Suffragan Bishop of Hull (1552) and Archdeacon of Nottingham (1553) who, by refusing to take the oath of Elizabeth I, was deprived of the living. He founded a grammar school in Tideswell, and another at Guisborough in Yorkshire where his name is inscribed in the parish church as the last Prior of the now ruined Priory. A very long epitaph on the brass monument on the chancel tells all in doggerel. It is surprising that this has survived, for it shows the prelate in complete Eucharistic vestments of Pre-Reformation style including his mitre and pastoral staff. He retained his bishopric in a most tenacious way, being consecrated in the reign of Protestant Edward VI, returned to Papist ways in the reign of Mary and even sat on a commission enquiring into heresies. He always maintained a dignified manner and, whilst in Guisborough, it was noted that 'he lived in a most sumptuous style'. When the Priory was suppressed in 1540, he retired on a handsome pension of £166.13.4 (£166.66) per annum. His monument is all the more interesting because less than a dozen brasses in the country commemorate bishops.

In the churchyard, a pedestal bearing a sundial marks the grave of William Newton, carpenter, poet and partner in the rebuilding (1815) and humane ownership of Cresswell Mill. Anna Seward, poetess of Lichfield, with whom Erasmus

Darwin had a friendly relationship, called Newton 'The Minstrel of the Peak'. Another minstrel, Samuel Slack (1822) is also buried here adjacent to the gateway leading to the vicarage. The headstone . . . 'was erected by the Voluntary contributions of the Barlow Choir and a few other admirers of that noble deep toned melodist'. Slack was brought to sing before the King but by all accounts, standing in such illustrious company did nothing to improve his rough and ready ways.

(Photograph: the author)

Sundial marks the grave of
William Newton

YOULGREAVE

All Saints was formally dedicated in 1224. Much of that original Norman building survives; additions or alterations do not detract in any way from its charm and general interest. Overtopped by an immensely strong and many pinnacled 15th century tower, surpassed only by All Saints, Derby, the church is a well known landmark to travellers in the Peak District, and some consider it to be the most impressive of its kind in the county.

Inside, the chest tomb of Thomas Cockayne (restored 1873) completes the medieval jigsaw of the family numerously represented in Ashbourne. Measuring only 36 by 18 inches, it has no record of the age of Thomas when he died or an explanation of the circumstances of his death. An altercation with Thomas Burdett occurred when the two men were on their way to church at Polesworth and, according to that story, Cockayne died because of a fall 'due to the unevenness of the ground'. The truth is a secret of the tomb. His head rests on a helmet surmounted by a cock, the family crest, and over his plate armour there is a collar bearing the motif of the House of York. The monument is a fine example of delicate carving in alabaster.

Agnes, daughter of Thomas Barley of Barlow, aunt of the first husband of Bess of Hardwick, was herself the wife of Thomas Cockayne. He left her with several children, notably Thomas, later known as 'The Magnificent' interred at Ashbourne. His daughter Elizabeth married Robert Burdett, a descendant of the man with whom Thomas Cockayne is said to have quarrelled.

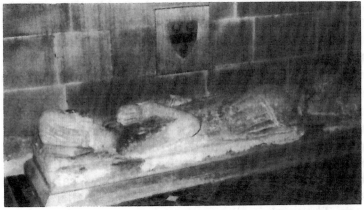

(Photograph: the author)

The oldest massive effigy is believed to be of Sir John Rossington, resting cross-legged with a heart in his hands. It's great age can hardly be disputed for it wears a quilted coat (now very worn) of 12th or 13th century style. The Rossingtons were powerful landowners connected by marriage to the Cockaynes and Gilberts. Robert Gilbert is remembered with his wife and seventeen children on either side of the Virgin and Child, beautifully carved out of a sadly damaged alabaster slab, on which the general sense of movement is most attractive.

A brass recalls Frideswide, spinster member of the family who died in 1604. She was the third daughter of Francis Gilbert, a great great grandson of Robert mentioned above. The brass donated by her brother 'John Gilbert, a third son, marchant and taylor of Londo' (London) is of special interest because it gives an excellent idea of the costume worn by a Lady of quality in the reign of the first Elizabeth, and because it is the only monument of its kind here.

The clothes that made the man, and the opulence of the better off Elizabethans can be seen on the monument of Robert Rowe from nearby Alport, with his severe and rotund wife Katherine and their several children.

The 17th century poor often relied on charity or gifts, sometimes distributed through the local church, and this was the case in Youlgreave. A board, inside the west door, announces 'Mr. James Roberts of Alport left by His last will bearing date January 1st 1681 Forty Shillings to be yearly and every year for ever Distributed by the Vicar of Youlgreave . . . to ten of the most needy old men and ten of the poorest widows in Youlgreave and Alport upon Christmas Day'. And Mr. Samuel Robert of Alport (1752) 'settled the Payment . . . for Ever, upon three Pieces or Parcels of lands, one called Barearse Pingle, and the two others called the High Flat in the Parish of Youlgreave'.

Youlgreave's unique font is a large bowl carved with a mythical creature which appears to hold a smaller bowl in its mouth. The work is all one piece dating from about the 12th century. The purpose of the small bowl which has been extensively debated, is probably no more than a unique style of Holy Water stoup such as would have been found in any pre-Reformation church. The font came from Elton where it was rejected before being brought to Youlgreave to reside in the Vicarage garden for a time prior to being set up in the church in 1838, several centuries after the tiny pilgrim figure set into the north wall was fashioned by an ancient craftsman.

MELBOURNE

St. Mary's, Derbyshire's most complete Norman Church, which should be visited less for monuments than for its magnificent architecture, is a cruciform structure one hundred and twenty feet in length, of ancient but uncertain date and one of the rare churches to possess a narthex. The massive masonry is a true memorial to the stonemasons' skills. Pillars fifteen feet high and four in diameter, reach to the scalloped cushioned capitals commanding the eye to take in at one sweep the closely placed stilted arches, chevron tooled on one side, plain on the other, pressing upwards to the clerestory, triforium and seventeenth century roof which replaced the original steeply pitched cover, which style can still be found in parts of Northern France. At the crossing, each side rests on pillars with cushion capitals, some well decorated, others quite plain.

Parish churches with an apse, a semi-circular extension beyond the chancel, are uncommon in Derbyshire, yet Melbourne once boasted three including those at the altars in the transepts. These have unfortunately gone, swept away in the fifteenth century and now, there is only one example of the ancient builders' architectural style, All Saints Chapel, Steetley.

STEETLEY

J. C. Cox suggests that All Saints was built shortly after the Domesday Survey, either by Gley de Briton or one of his sons who held the land.

It is a little more than fifty feet by sixteen, the nave slightly wider than the chancel, terminating in an apse. The arch which divides the nave from the chancel is a delight, with capitals decorated with scrolls, leaf work, a lion with two heads, St. George, a hapless maiden and a dragon. In the apse, the ribs of the roof rise from decorated pillars, all quite detailed, of Adam, Eve and the serpent, and strange fishy creatures, all rising to terminate in an Agnus Dei medallion.

Thus the Christian concept of creation, good versus evil and eventual redemption are all beautifully demonstrated by the stone mason's art.

For almost three centuries this chapel was roofless, used as a cowbyre, store shed and hen house until restored to its former glory in 1870.

Describing Steetley chapel, Nikolaus Pevsner writes '. . . there are few Norman churches in England so consistently made into show pieces by those who designed them . . .' Dr. Cox goes further 'The building', he says, 'is quite a gem of architectural art . . . it is one of the most complete and beautiful specimens of Norman work on a small scale that can be met with anywhere in this country or in Normandy . . .'

The girdle which surrounds the exterior of the apse is the perfection of the mason's skill.

There is only one monument here, to Lawrence Le Leche, the priest at the time of the plague in 1349. He chose to be buried in the porch so that worshippers who passed over his interred body, would remember to pray for him.

ASHOVER

All Saints has a slender spire of 128 feet overtopping the towered, embattled and gargoyled church of various dates from the thirteenth century. The tower was built by the Babingtons in the fifteenth century.

On the chancel, a brass monument, a priest in Eucharistic vestments, commemorates Robert Eyre, the fifteenth century rector, son of Philip and grandson of Robert Eyre and John Padley of Hathersage. The Eyre and Reresby families were closely connected and between 1343 and 1529, seven Reresby sons were vicars here.

On the south side of the altar, another brass commemorates James Rolleston and his wife Anna, sister of Thomas Babington. Anna died in 1507. The date of James' demise is unknown but it was later than 1518 when he witnessed the will of Thomas Babington. The memorial also bears figures of nine daughters and four sons in simple tunics, unlike James who boasts a set of armour.

In the fourteenth century, the youngest son of Sir Ralph Rolleston bought the manor of Lea. The memorial records the buyer's grandson whose successors retained the manor until the reign of Elizabeth I.

The 'Babington Quire' screen is now gone, leaving only the table tomb of Thomas Babington and his wife Editha, sister of Sir Anthony Fitzherbert of Norbury. Editha died before Thomas who departed on 13th March 1518. He left instructions that Editha should not be disturbed and that he was to be laid by her side. Their coloured effigies show Thomas in civilian dress ornamented with a gypciere. His head rests on a pillow originally supported by angels. Editha, no less grand in her close fitting gown and square head-dress, wears rings on each hand. Around the sides of the tomb are several small figures which help to make this memorial one of the finest listed in this booklet.

The extensive Babington family came to Derbyshire from East Bridgeford before the battle of Agincourt (1415) when Thomas Babington, 63, married Isabella, heiress of Robert Dethick. Babington sold his patrimony to Sir William, his youngest brother, Chief Baron of the Exchequer under Henry II.

John was the eldest son of Thomas and Isabella and he married Isabell Bradbourne whose family are remembered in the Boothby Chapel in Saint Oswald's, Ashbourne. John, who was the father of Thomas and Anna mentioned above, was killed at the battle of Bosworth Field (1485).

Fixed to the wall at the foot of the Babington monument there is a palimpsest, now hinged so both sides may be read. The face recalls the Babington but the reverse is a memorial to Robert Prykke who was Sergeant of the Pantry to Queen Margaret and does not seem to have any connection with Ashover.

The mural to Guilielm Dakeyn 'King of Arms' was probably altered by his grandson to bring some credit to the ancestor, famed as a forger and pedlar of cut price pedigrees, who was pilloried and had an ear cut off for these offences, in 1592.

'The most important Norman font in the county' is how Pevsner describes the small lead bowl in this church. It is decorated all around with tiny figures, and stands on a plinth (1866). As there are very few lead fonts in England (Cromwell smelted them down for ammunition) it is of special interest.

There is no glass of great age in this church.

DERBY

All Saints was elevated to Cathedral status in 1927. Its pride is the magnificent sixteenth century tower in the Perpendicular style which reaches to one hundred and seventy four feet below the pinnacles. It was once described as '. . . a prince amongst subjects, a giant amongst dwarfs . . .' The west door, under the tower immediately beyond Bakewell's iron gates, leads into the church proper, rebuilt in 1723-25 and extended at the east end in recent years.

Dr. Michael Hutchinson took office in Derby in 1719, six years after a parish meeting advised the Corporation '. . . All St. chancell w'ch they aught to prepare is much out of repare. And all Sts church is much out of repare and aught to be repared by the parish', and requested that a brief for repair should be obtained from the Queen.

This raised only £500 so the project was dropped, but Dr. Hutchinson took the law into his own hands, opened the church to his workmen during the night of 18th February 1723 and by morning all, except the tower was razed. Subscriptions for rebuilding began. The Doctor, a persuasive collector, allowed nobody to escape his net but insufficient money was produced. He auctioned seat places to raise £500 and a storm of protest. He weathered that by handing in his resignation and withdrew it when he learnt who his successor was. Anger came to the boil on Sunday 16th April 1727 when the Mayor and Corporation, attended by the Mace Bearer, ordered their appointee to take the pulpit in place of Dr. Hutchinson's appointed deputy. The brawl that erupted caused the Mayor to be summoned before the Ecclesiastical Court, and Hutchinson received an eviction notice. Twelve months later, the imperious Doctor left town. He is quite sadly remembered only by a discreet mural on the south wall, almost obscured by the bookstall.

The new church, designed by Gibbs, was opened in 1725. Many early monuments are lost; those that remain are dominated by Bess of Hardwick's which she designed, had built and frequently inspected before she died. It stands in the Cavendish chapel, beyond the iron screen and gates by Bakewell, Derbyshire's most famous Blacksmith and artist in wrought iron. Bess was an energetic and rapacious lady whose first ambition was to enhance the status of her children by the acquisition of wealth. Her first husband, Robert Barley, married her when she was fourteen, called her 'beautiful and discreet', died without issue and left his entire estate to her. She was thirty years old on the 20th August 1547 when Sir William Cavendish took her to wife at two o'clock in the morning, at Bradgate. Under her spell, the Treasurer of the Chamber of Henry VIII, began the building of Chatsworth House, gave her the fruits of a fairly happy marriage, six children including the sons of Edensor, and died in October 1557. His place was taken by William St. Lo, Grand Butler of England, Captain of Queen Elizabeth's Guard, a man of substance and ardour who, before he died in 1565, sold his southern England estates to purchase lands in Derbyshire for 'Sweet Chatsworth', all to the exclusion of his other family.

George Talbot, sixth Earl of Shrewsbury, widower of Gertrude, daughter of the first Earl of Rutland, was the next to fall to her charms. Bess chose to wife him in 1568, after keeping him a-dangling until he agreed that his eldest son, Gilbert (by Gertrude) would take Bess's daughter Mary to wife, whilst his daughter Grace married her eldest son

Henry, with 'suitable settlements'.

George Talbot, her most ambitious and important catch was dubbed. Knight of the Garter in 1561 and later appointed warden of Mary Queen of Scots. Then, a hitherto harmonious marriage deteriorated into recriminations and bitterness. The situation worsened when Bess offended the Queen by marrying off one of her daughters to the Earl of Lennox, and found herself in the Tower for daring to bring her family too near to the throne. Shrewsbury made several representations on her behalf, but she had three months to think about her rashness. Family affection had been undermined. The Queen herself became involved and finally Shrewsbury went to live at Hansworth Park where he ended his days in 1590 in the care of a rapacious housemaid. He is buried in Sheffield parish church.

Bess lived on for seventeen years, finished building Hardwick Hall, Oldcoates, and the less well known Almshouses in Full Street, Derby. She died immensely rich, with few friends on the 16th February 1607 or 1608, nearer to ninety years than the eighty she claimed, on a day of

Derby Cathedral

hard frost when her masons could not work, to fulfill a prophesy that she would not die whilst she was building.

Also in the Cavendish chapel, are white marble busts to the Earl and Countess of Bessborough, and several coffin plates to members of the Cavendish family. Forty are interred here including scientist Henry Cavendish who found conversation and women superfluous, wore the same shovel hat for forty years and is known internationally by the Cambridge laboratory named after him.

There is also a wooden effigy thought to be the 16th century Sub-Dean Johnson, and across the chancel, memorials recall William Allestry (1655) Recorder of Derby, and Thomas Chambers, (1726) a London merchant who donated £100 to Dr. Hutchinson.

The oldest monument in the church is an incised alabaster tombstone to Johannes Low (1440).

MORLEY

One of the county's prettiest parish churches is St. Mathews of Morley. It contains a fine selection of monumental brasses and other memorials, which allows the visitor a fascinating insight to the history of the building and its benefactors.

The village was little known until Richard de Morley's great grand-daughter Goditha married Ralph Stathum and brought the Morley property to her husband. It is from their lifetime that the present church building is dated. Ralph Stathum who came of Cheshire stock was a Derbyshire Knight in the reign of Richard II. He took down the Norman aisle and had it rebuilt. Goditha continued the work when he died in 1380 and rebuilt what is now the south aisle and the roof.

There are two brasses, both in Latin, recording the alterations effected by this couple, the first is to Ralph and the second to Goditha tells that the building they undertook was completed in 1403.

Ralph and Goditha had two children: Richard who died quite young, recorded on the plate to his mother as an associate in her building endeavours. The second son, Thomas, has no memorial. He married Elizabeth, daughter of Robert Lumley, and their son John took to wife Cecily Cornwall. The latter couple are commemorated on three brasses. The first is a plate inscribed in Latin 'Orate p'aia John Stathum Armiger . . . et . . . Cecille . . .'. The second, in the paving of the north aisle, is important because it is the earliest brass protraiture in the church. John kneels on a helmet, wears 15th century armour and his ungloved hands are joined in prayer. His wife kneels opposite him, and below the figures is an inscription in English. The final plate is very unusual, perhaps unique, for it asks for specifically named prayers to be offered for the 'Sowles of Rafe Godyth Thomas Elizabeth Cecill and John and of theyrs suxcessores and for all cristen Sowles'. Unfortunately, this is not in the church at this date.

Thomas, who was John's son, died in 1470. He married twice, firstly Elizabeth, daughter of Robert Langley, and secondly, Thomasina, daughter of John Curzon. All three are commemorated on a very skilfully decorated brass, on a table tomb in the vestry.

The next generation of Stathums is represented on a large brass, on the right of the high altar, to Henry and his three wives. The first two ladies look very much like the wives of Thomas but the third who survived her husband is more elaborately and stylishly gowned with a mantle fastened at the shoulders. The inscription tells us that the wives were Anna and Elizabeth, daughters of Thomas Bothe and Edgar Syclon respectively, and the third wife (on the left facing the brass) was Margaret, daughter of John Stanhope. Henry died on the 30th April 1480 and had four daughters and a son, but the only survivor and sole heiress, represented on the brass, was Joan who married John Sacheverall from Snitterton. His mother was a daughter of John Curzon of Kedleston. The brass momento, on the wall to the right of the priest's door in the vestry, shows John who died at the battle of Bosworth in 1485, with his three sons, and opposite them Joan with five daughters.

After Bosworth, Joan married William Zouch. The sons of John and Joan Sacheverell were John who died early in his youth, Henry and Ralph. The latter is the ancestor of the Sacheverells of Radcliffe on Soar.

Henry of Morley (1558) married twice, Isabella, daughter of Sir John Montgomery of Cubley who is shown with him on the brass memorial where Isabella's gown fuller and more elaborate than on any brass here, shows a considerable change in fashion. His second wife, Margaret Holford, is not recorded on the Sacheverell brass.

Of the eight children of a first marriage, only one has a monument here, the effigy of Katherine, who married Thomas Babington of Dethick. She was the grandmother of Anthony Babington executed in 1586 for plotting against Queen Elizabeth I.

The monument to Henry Sacheverell's great great grandson Jacynth in the north chapel bears his effigy and that of his wife Elizabeth, daughter of Sir Richard Harper of Littleover. Jacynth died in 1646, thirty years after he erected the almshouses for the poor of Morley and Smalley.

Following the Reformation, this family, despite many hardships, rigorously adhered to the Catholic Faith. The inscription on Jacynth's tomb clearly states this, so it seems likely that it must have been added, at the earliest, after the Commonwealth. Jacynth's brother, Jonathan, was the first member of the family to embrace the Protestant religion. His monument in the south aisle announces that he was 'the last of the eldest line of the Sacheverells of Morley in Derbyshire who died a true Protestant, VII day of November 1662, the 79 year of his age'.

His wife is also figured here and two children. Both died in infancy.

At the head of Jacynth's tomb, four incised slabs in the floor are to Henry who, at nineteen and five months, died five weeks after his wedding, to Ralph a year and five months old (1635), to Richard buried in Sutton Coldfield, and to Dorothy who died on 20th January 1639 when she was sixteen years and two months.

The two windows in the north side of the north aisle were presented to Morley Church by Francis Pole in 1529. He obtained them from the Refectory of Dale Abbey near Ilkeston, which was broken up during the Dissolution of the Monastries. The glasswork was faithfully restored by Warrington of London in 1847.

In one window the legend of St. Robert the Hermit is depicted in 7 panels, with an inscription in each. The eighth compartment shows an erring monk being told 'Take heed of thy ways, brother'. This panel probably came from another window. Dr. Cox quotes a source which suggests that it may refer to an incident in the life of Henry, an early Prior of Dale, whom the Abbot of Tupholme ordered to be brought before him by force, for his continued disobedience and misconduct with a certain young woman of Morley.

The bottom panels contain the arms of Dale Abbey, Francis Pole, the Bateman, and the Sitwell families.

The next important window in the east corner of the north chapel, tells in ten panels of the search for and finding of the true Cross.

The Derbyshire Heritage Series -

THE WATER CURE by Alan Bower
WOMEN OF DERBYSHIRE by Susan Watson
WORK & PLAY - Derbyshire, a photographic record - by Alan Bower
WRITERS WITH DERBYSHIRE CONNECTIONS by Jane Darrall
SPAGHETTI & BARBED WIRE - True World War II escapes story -
by Jack E. Fox
DERBYSHIRE GRAVES - 100 true and unusual graves - by Peter Naylor
ON THIS DAY....IN DERBYSHIRE - events that happened throughout the year - by John E. Heath
THE EARLS AND DUKES OF DEVONSHIRE by Julie Bunting
TIMMY GLASS WAISTCOAT - Early 20th century life in Clay Cross recalled - by Jack E. Fox
JOHN SMEDLEY of Matlock by John Large.
STORIES OF THE DERBYSHIRE DALES by John Large
JOSEPH PAXTON by John Large
DERBYSHIRE STAINED GLASS WINDOWS - by Dr. Joyce Critchlow
LOST VILLAGES OF DERBYSHIRE - by Peter Naylor
CROMFORD - A HISTORY - by Peter Naylor
THE WEAVERS KNOT - A weaver's tale by Rosie Ford
ELEGY OF AN EDWARDIAN CHILDHOOD IN DERBYSHIRE - Glossop area - by Ian Harlow
SPIT AND POLISH - Army life in Britain, India and Egypt during World War II - by Jack E. Fox
A PEAKLAND WILDLIFE YEAR by Richard Bunting
COUNTRY POETRY by Leslie Williamson
LOOK BACK AT LOSCOE by George Mellor
NORMAN & MEDIEVAL DERBYSHIRE by Richard Bunting
THE CIVIL WAR IN THE TRENT VALLEY by Andrew Polkey
A WIRKSWORTH BOYHOOD - 1941 - 1958 by Max Hodnett
A WIRKSWORTH WELL REMEMBERED by Eric Repton
ILKESTON TRAMS & TROLLEYBUSES by John David Watts
A LONG EATON BOYHOOD by Alan Neatby-Smith

OTHER JOHN MERRILL WALK BOOKS

For a free complete catalogue of John Merrill walk Guides send a SAE to The John Merrill Foundation

**Visit our website -
www.walkinglondon.org**

THE LITTLE JOHN CHALLENGE WALK
YORKSHIRE DALES CHALLENGE WALK
NORTH YORKSHIRE MOORS CHALLENGE WALK
LAKELAND CHALLENGE WALK
THE RUTLAND WATER CHALLENGE WALK
MALVERN HILLS CHALLENGE WALK
THE SALTER'S WAY
THE SNOWDON CHALLENGE
CHARNWOOD FOREST CHALLENGE WALK
THREE COUNTIES CHALLENGE WALK (Peak District).
CAL-DER-WENT WALK by Geoffrey Carr,
THE QUANTOCK WAY
BELVOIR WITCHES CHALLENGE WALK
THE CARNEDDAU CHALLENGE WALK
THE SWEET PEA CHALLENGE WALK
THE LINCOLNSHIRE WOLDS - BLACK DEATH - CHALLENGE WALK
JENNIFER'S CHALLENGE WALK
THE EPPING FOREST CHALLENGE WALK
THE THREE BOROUGH CHALLENGE WALK - NORTH LONDON

INSTRUCTION & RECORD -
HIKE TO BE FIT......STROLLING WITH JOHN
THE JOHN MERRILL WALK RECORD BOOK
HIKE THE WORLD - John Merrill's guide to walking & Backpacking.

MULTIPLE DAY WALKS -
THE RIVERS'S WAY
PEAK DISTRICT: HIGH LEVEL ROUTE
PEAK DISTRICT MARATHONS
THE LIMEY WAY
THE PEAKLAND WAY
COMPO'S WAY by Alan Hiley
THE BRIGHTON WAY by Norman Willis

THE PILGRIM WALKS SERIES -
THE WALSINGHAM WAY - ELY TO WALSINGHAM - 72 MILES
THE WALSINGHAM WAY - Kings Lynn to Walsingham - 35 miles
TURN LEFT AT GRANJA DE LA MORERUELA - 700 MILES
NORTH TO SANTIAGO DE COMPOSTELA, VIA FATIMA - 650 miles
St. OLAV'S WAY - Oslo to Trondheim - 400 miles
St. WINEFRIDE'S WAY - St. Asaph to Holywell
St. ALBANS WAY - Waltham Abbey to St. Albans - 26 miles
St. KENELM TRAIL by John Price - Clent Hills to Winchcombe - 60 miles
DERBYSHIRE PILGRIMAGES
LONDON TO CANTERBURY- 83 MILES

COAST WALKS & NATIONAL TRAILS -
ISLE OF WIGHT COAST PATH
PEMBROKESHIRE COAST PATH
THE CLEVELAND WAY
WALKING ANGELSEY'S COASTLINE.
WALKING THE COASTLINE OF THE CHANNEL ISLANDS
THE ISLE OF MAN COASTAL PATH - "THE WAY OF THE GULL."
A WALK AROUND HAYLING ISLAND
A WALK AROUND THE ISLE OF SHEPPEY

DERBYSHIRE & PEAK DISTRICT HISTORICAL GUIDES -
A TO Z GUIDE OF THE PEAK DISTRICT
DERBYSHIRE INNS - an A to Z guide
HALLS AND CASTLES OF THE PEAK DISTRICT & DERBYSHIRE
TOURING THE PEAK DISTRICT & DERBYSHIRE BY CAR
DERBYSHIRE FOLKLORE
PUNISHMENT IN DERBYSHIRE
CUSTOMS OF THE PEAK DISTRICT & DERBYSHIRE
WINSTER - a souvenir guide
ARKWRIGHT OF CROMFORD
LEGENDS OF DERBYSHIRE
DERBYSHIRE FACTS & RECORDS
TALES FROM THE MINES by Geoffrey Carr
PEAK DISTRICT PLACE NAMES by Martin Spray
DERBYSHIRE THROUGH THE AGES - Vol 1 -DERBYSHIRE IN PREHISTORIC TIMES
SIR JOSEPH PAXTON
FLORENCE NIGHTINGALE
JOHN SMEDLEY
BONNIE PRINCE CHARLIE & 20 MILE WALK.
THE STORY OF THE EARLS AND DUKES OF DEVONSHIRE

JOHN MERRILL'S MAJOR WALKS -
TURN RIGHT AT LAND'S END
WITH MUSTARD ON MY BACK
TURN RIGHT AT DEATH VALLEY
EMERALD COAST WALK
I CHOSE TO WALK - Why I walk etc.
A WALK IN OHIO - 1,310 MILES AROUND THE BUCKEYE TRAIL.

SKETCH BOOKS -
SKETCHES OF THE PEAK DISTRICT

COLOUR BOOK:-
THE PEAK DISTRICT.......SOMETHING TO REMEMBER HER BY.

OVERSEAS GUIDES -
HIKING IN NEW MEXICO - Vol I - The Sandia and Manzano Mountains.
Vol 2 - Hiking "Billy the Kid" Country. Vol 4 - N.W. area - " Hiking Indian Country."
"WALKING IN DRACULA COUNTRY" - Romania.
WALKING THE TRAILS OF THE HONG KONG ISLANDS.

VISITOR GUIDES - MATLOCK . BAKEWELL. ASHBOURNE.